OPEN HEART
OPEN ARMS

WELCOMING MIGRANTS TO IRELAND

ALAN HILLIARD

First published in 2016 by Messenger Publications

ISBN 978 1 910248 48 5

Designed by Messenger Publications Design Department
Typeset in Times New Roman and Charlemagne Std
Printed by W & G Baird Ltd

MESSENGER
PUBLICATIONS
JESUITS in IRELAND

Messenger Publications,
37 Lower Leeson Street, Dublin 2
www.messenger.ie

DEDICATION

This publication coincides with the 30th anniversary
of my ordination to priesthood.

I'd like to dedicate this work to those who helped
me mark the occasion during this significant year,
especially those who were present in body, mind,
soul or spirit on the Flaggy Shore in Clare in July.

The words of Seamus Heaney best describe the
impact of this occasion on my being: it is times like
this that '*catch the heart off guard and blow it open*'.
I am forever grateful to you all.

Alan

ACKNOWLEDGEMENTS

I'd like to acknowledge the editor of Messenger Publications, Donal Neary SJ, for his confidence in my ability to produce this resource, and his team for their professional attention at every stage of the publication. I would also like to thank Suzanne Greene, Peggy Doherty, Noirin Lynch, Karen McHugh and Patricia Kennedy for their efficient and effective feedback along the way. I'd like to especially thank Bobby Gilmore for his constant support in this most important mission.

The Third World is knocking on our doors, and it will come in even if we are not in agreement[1].

INTRODUCTION

I watched a family arrive to a private housing estate in a Dublin suburb, which lies inside the M50. I knew the house had been purchased recently by the HSE and many were wondering who would take possession of the property.

They arrived without notice and nobody knew if they were from Afghanistan, Iraq, Pakistan, Syria or Sudan. There was no induction, no welcome or no knock on the door to say to people 'these are your new neighbours'. Maybe people want it that way. Maybe neighbours don't want to take on any more; they've reared their children and they just want to take it easy now. Maybe the newly arrived family just want to keep their heads down, afraid of suspicion or harassment, or just plain old misunderstandings. Maybe some would rather have distance and walls between people, reflecting the more individualised lifestyles in today's society, compared to the dense community upbringings of previous days in Dublin, when local communities challenged institutional apathy or arrogance.

As I watched, the father took his young child by the hand, to walk to the shop. The sight of the proud father and the skipping child brought back to me the days my father took me for a 'treat' – the happy skip anticipating a surprise or a pre-negotiated ice-cream, chocolate bar, or even the latest soccer player cards that I fixed into the ever more bulging First Division team album.

I was once a stranger in that same street when I first moved there as a four year old from my grandfather's house. When we came home from England, my grandfather opened his heart, his arms and his home to us. He gave us shelter while the foundation was set and the bricks were laid for our new home.

Exodus 22:23 reads: a*nd you shall not wrong a stranger or oppress them, for you were strangers in the land of Egypt*. And so I was a stranger who found a home. There were always strangers; there was always some other 'gang' who was the enemy. They became friends because parents introduced us, or we arrived into the same classroom, or we joined the same soccer team. All of these friendships and associations enriched me as I grew towards maturity regardless of how long they lasted. Years on, as I watched this young child with his father, I remembered how I too was a stranger once.

OPENING OUR HEARTS

This booklet is published by Messenger Publications, who bring us *The Sacred Heart Messenger* magazine. As such it is a religious publication steeped in Catholic thought, tradition and ethos. This specific publication, entitled *Open Heart, Open Arms*, highlights the rich and insightful pastoral teaching of the Catholic Church on migration. As we listen to the news, read our newspapers and follow stories on various social media and internet sites, we find ourselves thinking thoughts that others plant in our minds. The purpose of this booklet is to situate our minds and hearts in our rich tradition of faith, thus allowing us to think with a noble Christian mind and heart, rather than some of the less Christian narratives we are confronted with regarding this issue.

If local communities are to assist with migrant integration, there are two main points to focus their work. These points are highlighted in the Magna Carta of the Church's teaching on migration, which was published in 2004 by The Pontifical Council for the Pastoral Care of Migrants and Itinerant People, entitled *Erga Migrantes Caritas Christi,* or in English, *The Love of Christ for Migrants* (EMCC)[2]. Firstly EMCC states that there are two welcomes. There is the first welcome which is the welcome that assists immediate accommodation needs, support for people in transit etc. The subsequent welcomes are to be part of a strategy that aims at the 'progressive integration and self-sufficiency of the immigrant' (EMCC para. 43). This welcome, which goes beyond the first welcome, also involves helping people stay in touch with their homeland, should the opportunity for return become possible. The second welcome is much more strategic, whereby the immigrant is not the focus of a community's charity, but it does involve helping the immigrant feel a part of the life of the community; 'Religious, social, charitable and cultural associations of Christian inspiration should also make efforts to involve immigrants themselves in their (local Church) structures'. Furthermore, this will help immigrants cultivate a sense of responsibility toward their new home and will help them move into a participative culture and will further assist moving people from a dependency culture. In some countries, a culture of dependency has allowed people stay stuck in a comfort trap where they do not use, or are inhibited in their use of, their skills that in normal circumstances would allow them to progress and integrate into society.

The second principle governing engagement is that the local Church must remember that as the community responds to migrants, these actions are not undertaken to proselytise those of other faiths. *Erga Migrantes* reminds us that within the ethics of meeting others we must always be 'respecting differences and practising solidarity' (EMCC 102). Similarly Pope Francis 'tweeted' on 6 June 2016 that: 'We need to discover the gifts of each person: may communities transmit their own values and be open to the differences in others'[3].

As Catholics, the presence of the migrants reveals to us the changing nature of society today and we are tasked to live accordingly. We are asked to 'overcome prejudices and biases' in order to see the 'multi-ethnic, intercultural and multi-religious nature of our ever changing world' (EMCC 100). Never again will the world be a purely homogenised place of one culture; the challenge to people of faith is to know their own faith and live it well in the face of diversity; this environment is similar to the one that Jesus knew in Galilee. The language of the state is the language of integration and cohesion but for people of faith the language is building fraternity and communion within the community of faith as at Pentecost.

The ultimate aim of this booklet is to help foster an understanding of the plight of migrants that leads to action in the local faith community. Understanding of the role of the Christian towards the ever more present reality of migration, and of the great Catholic tradition of hospitality is more important than ever, especially if we want to make the appropriate response. Hopefully this booklet will help to nurture the instincts of those who wish to make a difference as we constantly face the greatest crisis in Europe since the Second World War. A man I know who is a refugee of the Balkan conflict said he prays every day for migrants; he knows the pain of their journey.

This booklet has three main sections, the first of which, *Migration and the Migrant*, helps us to understand some of the labels we use in the face of the present crisis. Each word used by media, by politicians, by people in pubs and others in this debate is loaded with emotion and misunderstandings. It is hoped that the reader will understand these labels through different eyes, thus adopting alternative vistas on what many in today's world see through the lens of an inconvenience. The terms 'migration' and 'migrants' are seen by some as a rude interruption of their lives, which echoes the 'globalised indifference' that Pope Francis spoke about during his visit to Lampedusa in July 2013.

The second section explores some Old and New Testament insights into the migrant journey and the context within which diversity is seen as an important part of Gospel living. The scriptural analysis is addressed within the Churches' teaching on migration and also looks at hospitality within an important historical and lively aspect of Christian life. The third section looks at the challenge that faces us as we try to respond to the needs of those who come to our land as refugees. A lot of emphasis is placed on the disposition that we foster through an understanding of the first two sections. Once this disposition is in place, the response unfolds quite easily and naturally.

I make one appeal to you the reader. When discussing matters relating to 'Church', there is one consistent difficulty, which is to define specifically what 'Church' one is talking about. Hopefully it will be clear to you whether it is the local Church, the National Church, the teaching authority of the Church, or the Church of the two or three who are meeting in His name that is being referred to at each and every juncture.

MIGRATION AND THE MIGRANT

In order for there to be nothing to worry about, the managers of the global order need an inexhaustible abundance of local unrest[4].

WHAT IS MIGRATION?

Migration for many centuries was a way of life rather than a problem to be solved. From the earliest times, people were nomadic. Their home was determined by the seasons. Planting, feeding, safety, and climate determined where home was at any particular point in time. Cities and towns, where they existed, were places of trade. But among the nomadic peoples trade was somewhat minimised as most people had enough to live on.

Migration is not new and migration between Northern Europe and Africa is definitely not new. Records in the eighth century show that there was a vibrant trade between North Africa and Germany, which, ironically, is not unlike today's movement of peoples. Paul the Deacon writing in the eighth century described how slaves were sent back to Africa because German people were prolific at bearing children to the extent that he reckoned the name Germany came from the Latin term *Germania*, which means to germinate! They sold their slaves onto Southern Europe but they also sold them back to Africa, as the Arab world was desperate for workers when plagues wiped out the population. People travelled as far north as Utrecht and Venice to purchase slaves. Amazingly, the value of a slave tripled from the time they were abducted from Africa to the time they were resold at the German markets at a later stage[5].

This short overview highlights the vibrancy of migration and indeed trafficking between Northern Europe and Northern Africa as far back as the eighth century. This form of migration may be termed as organised or forced migration, where business interests in need of labour look outside their normal labour supply to find willing hands to meet the demand of their specific businesses at that time. Some forms of migration paid little heed to the plight of the person who was forced to migrate at the hands of those who plundered or trafficked them.

There are many other forms of migration when migrants choose to travel freely and are presented with opportunities abroad attracting them away from the place they once called home. Ireland is familiar with this aspect of migration. It is not unusual to find articles in the *Irish Times Generation Emigration* website outlining the pros and cons of individual migrations. Titles such as *Life Abroad: Emigrating to Australia was the best decision I have ever made[6]*, capture the wonder, ecstasy, struggle and the oftentimes confusion of those who seek a better life abroad.

The economist John Kenneth Galbraith, in his 1979 book *The Nature of Mass Poverty*, described migration as "the oldest action against poverty", and so it is. Everyone wants a piece of the cake; those who travel think by going somewhere else they get a bigger slice and those who attract them need an increased labour force to increase their share of the cake. However the term 'poverty' that

Galbraith referred to in this definition need not be solely economic poverty. Many migrants move today because of a mental, emotional, spiritual or social poverty. However, this should not take away from the fact that many move because they have nothing where they once lived, where their life is in danger and where they cannot protect those they love. It is in this spirit that we move onto our next section as one cannot define or understand migration fully without considering the plight of those who migrate.

WHAT IS A MIGRANT?

I loved soccer when I was a child. There was nothing more exciting than a World Cup Tournament. In the days before the Republic of Ireland made their way to qualifying games, the focus was on England and Scotland and sometimes Wales. In the 1970s and '80s, the strangest name in football was Peter Bonetti, the Chelsea goalkeeper. Despite his strange sounding name, he was born in Putney, London. The weekly fixtures highlighted on *Match of the Day* and *The Big Match* on Sunday afternoons were totally provincial. Unlike today, most players were born in the British Isles. But when the World Cup was broadcast, the world opened up for me – the teams I was familiar with played in the opening rounds against countries I never knew existed. The internet was a long way off, so I had to find an atlas to discover their exact location in our world.

In the main, Irish people could travel to mainland England and, once they fulfilled certain criteria, within a matter of days could register for work and find accommodation. There was a time in the early eighties in Britain when the housing provision of local councils was very generous and many Irish benefited from this scheme, as they did from other benefits that were available.

Europe was easy because once you travelled east there was one big spot called USSR, and geography lessons in school taught me the countries comprising Europe, which was a considerably smaller number than the number of countries in today's Europe. Africa was neatly squared off and South and Central America were judged by me on their proximity to Brazil, the great footballing nation in that era and most importantly the home of Pelé. As a child I thought that these national lines were fixed from the beginning of time, however as I grew older I soon began to realise that these countries were the constructs of various forces and powers.

Within these various constructs called countries, people lived. Over time, they created unique cultures, societies and communities. These people had rights accruing to them because of their attachment to this location. Rights varied from place to place and from space to space. In some spaces people had the right to engage in business and make what was called profits. Some others had no rights to profit but were promised the protection of the state from the cradle to the grave. Others had very little rights other than to the ground they stood on with restricted access to food, water, a job and housing, rights that were considered necessary and even obligatory in other jurisdictions. Others had what others called 'basic human rights' continuously infringed by gangs or unjust or uncaring regimes that were sometimes acting in the name of the government that supposedly took care of the space and of the people between the lines.

Anyone who crosses these lines for a period of time is

technically a migrant. They lose their official migrant status when they return back to the space between those lines or they undergo a process whereby the space they arrive into adopts them in one form or another and gives them rights. This explanation may be termed simplistic by many, but in essence it is the crossing of borders that creates migrants as far as the powers who govern these spaces are concerned.

What this overarching theory does not give consideration to, is what is termed 'internal migrants'. That is, people who travel within these spaces. As of April 2014, there were an estimated 232 million migrants world-wide and on top of this is a figure of 740 million internal migrants[7]. For instance someone who travelled from Kilrush in County Clare to Dublin for work or study would never have been considered a migrant in popular language or culture, but in essence they manifest the same reasons for leaving one place and moving to another as another person who crosses over the lines that we now call borders. There may be less challenges in a move within a country e.g. in language or customs but there are similar emotional and social wrenches. This distinction is important because present estimates tell us that when a migrant moves from Ballybofey to Ballybough or from Cahirciveen to Chicago they experience similar gains and losses. The hope is that the gains for the migrant outweigh the losses but both are always present.

A migrant is someone who enters new spaces in the hope that the gains in the new space outweigh the losses on leaving the old space they occupied both for themselves and their families. This fact is outlined very clearly in various narratives. The Kenyan-born Somali poet Warsan Shire tells us about the migrant:

you have to understand,
that no one puts their children in a boat
unless the water is safer than the land
no one burns their palms
under trains
beneath carriages
no one spends days and nights in the stomach of a
truck
feeding on newspaper unless the miles travelled
means something more than journey[8].

The hope and prayer for the migrant is that the welcome clamour of the new space can help drown out the sounds of the place that is left behind. This is the heartfelt prayer of all those many migrants who are represented behind the large numbers quoted by global agencies and it is alluded to in scripture. However it is not true in all cases; the exception is of course those who are trafficked illegally and against their will. Their desire is to be back in the place they came from as the place they are trafficked to represents fear and exploitation.

A REFUGEE

The year 2016 marked one hundred years since a group of people declared their intent to establish an Irish Republic and advocated for an independent nation and a move away from their colonial relationship with England. In all that occurred following this event, including a War of Independence and Civil War, there were very little restrictions on people travelling between Ireland and England. In the main, Irish people could travel to mainland England and within a matter of days register for work and find accommodation. Most even qualified automatically for welfare benefits. There were occasions in the 1980s whereupon an Irish person could literally arrive in London, register with the council and be automatically entitled to benefits. Despite political activism by a number of Irish in Britain and the, at times, strained political climate during the 'Troubles', at no stage did Britain limit the freedom of movement of the large and available workforce in the Republic of Ireland and Northern Ireland. Not all countries that had a historical link with Britain enjoyed this privilege.

In 1961, Ireland recorded its lowest ever population at 2.8 million. In 1959 and 1961 respectively, 64,494 and 72,962 new insurance cards were issued to immigrants from the Irish republic alone[9]. This relationship between Britain and Ireland overlaps with a colonial history. For many hundreds of years, aided by armies and navies, Britain took countries under its rule. Ireland, as a neighbour, created a tactical problem for the colonial power. At times, in the evolution of the colonies, and in the face of many wars, Ireland had to be 'discouraged' from establishing liaisons with countries such as Spain, France and Germany. Other countries stretching across Africa, the Americas, and the West Indies were part of these grand schemes, however the people in these 'colonies' did not enjoy the same freedoms as Irish people, who travelled between Ireland and Britain.

Under the British Nationality Act of 1948, Britain granted dual citizenship to anyone who was a citizen of a colony. In summary, anyone who was a member of Britain or its colonies was entitled to be a member of any of those countries. Over time, however, this changed. Countries like Canada decided to state who they would allow into their country.

In 1961, when the movement of Irish people to Britain was at its height, there was a strange contrast between the treatment of immigrants from different colonies, whereby the: 'employees of a bus company could go on strike if the company took on a 'coloured' conductor, bank managers could explain that they could not employ 'coloured' tellers because their customers would not like it'[10].

This same year saw great upset among the general population that a 'racial problem' was becoming ever more present. The Queen's speech that year announced a bill to manage immigration from Commonwealth countries. From that day to this, every government in Britain has promised to get tough on immigration. The recent Brexit debate highlighted this continuing trend. However, in the 1960s, there were instances of children arriving in airports, and a minister promising that he would 'get rid of them', without any dissenting voice being heard against this stance, which was a breach of basic humanitarian standards. While these decisions were made Irish children travelled freely between Ireland and England and many worked illegally without insurance cards. In 1968 an act was introduced by the British Parliament to issue a quota system on certain countries such as those in East Africa for fear that there would be a flood from former colonies. Initially, this quota stood at 1,500 a year and this was increased to 3,000 in 1971. There were no such restrictions placed on Irish people[11].

This shift in policy from equal access for former colonies to heavily restricted access did not remain unchallenged by circumstances. Situations arose in the former colonies that reawakened the moral responsibility allied with former colonial power. The Ugandan Crisis of

1972 meant that those of Asian origin who lived in Uganda were given three months to leave the country or face death. As a former colony this cohort of people had recourse only to Great Britain, who eventually admitted 27,000 people deemed to be refugees[12]. This situation reveals that restrictive immigration policies cannot compete with the moral obligation that exists towards our fellow brothers and sisters who experience difficulty – unless of course we choose to ignore their plight. In a world where there is political instability and poverty, there will always be refugees.

The 1951 UNHCR and the Refugee Convention were set up primarily to settle people who were dislodged following the fallout from the Second World War. Designed to give comfort and support to those based in Europe they were never intended to embrace the problems of migration that faces the world today. Migration in the 1950s was essential from east to west; migration from south to north was largely unknown in the offices that sculpted these new agreements. The terms for Asylum Seekers were outlined in the 1951 convention as well. Basically, an Asylum Seeker is one who seeks international protection and whose claim for refugee status has not yet been determined. The mind of the legislators at the time considered only people who sought asylum from behind the iron curtain. Anyone who defected reinforced the sense of a superior civilisation of the West, so once a person made their way to 'the West' from the Soviet bloc, they were automatically granted asylum. Again, in the mind of those who wrote the conventions, the focus was on east-west migration. The mind-set of the group that constructed these policies had not considered the huge increase in asylum applications as a result of a shift in the migratory flow from a historical east-west axis to a south-north axis.

Some might consider that this overview is a little patchy and inconsistent. Let's be honest migration policy is seldom the subject of planning; it is mostly a 'catch-up' exercise that is highly reactionary, except when a country wants to use migration and migrants to its advantage. We need look no further than the present crisis in the Mediterranean to understand this.

CONTEMPORARY POLICY RESPONSES TO MIGRATION AND MIGRANTS

As the divisions in our world became more obvious and wars, famines and disasters came to our attention on our TV screens and newspapers, we became all too familiar with the sights of refugee camps and the assistance provided by aid agencies. People were held in conditions that deprived them of many of the basic necessities of life. Today however, people won't sit around for too long. Reports from refugee camps tell of continuing conflicts within the camps and, being more aware of the outside world due to the internet and mobile phone services, camp inhabitants want the right to keep moving towards a humane destination. They want to move to a place where the perceived benefits outweigh their experiences of loss. In the world of migration the losses are termed 'push factors' i.e. things that push a person from the place they call home. 'Pull factors' also have an influence on migratory patterns. Increased interest in the attraction of much talked about locations in faraway cities; photographs on Facebook and other social media platforms are all 'pull factors' that continue to entice people away from their homelands. Furthermore, the development of the airline industry has made it easier to get to other countries than in times gone by.

Pull factors were very strong in Ireland's history of emigration. In the 1950s the last of the inhabitants of the Blasket Islands left their homes after the island was deemed uninhabitable by Government. The visitors to the island in previous decades opened the young islanders' minds to the world beyond their immediate horizon. Speaking on national radio, the author Críostóir Ó Floinn referred to the young islanders saying:

> The young women weren't willing to settle down anyplace there (…) They were going off to London as nurses, or going off to the civil service in Dublin, or anywhere. They wanted to go to the cities, got to America, if they could. You wouldn't blame them, you know[13].

As our world became a global village, various mechanisms were put in place to manage or at least to try to control the inevitable and increasing migration that was occurring via ever changing 'push' and 'pull' factors.

According to Michael Dummett[14], a great British philosopher of the 20th century, three tools have been developed to discourage migration, or, as some governments might say, to 'assist' migration. Firstly, Western countries have introduced visas, which have to be applied for before a person leaves their country of origin: a near impossible task if one is fleeing for one's life. This development tool has given rise to what some euphemistically call 'irregular migration' or 'the undocumented', who are basically people in a country without a visa. Human trafficking, people smugglers and criminal gangs are constantly trying to find ways to secure visas under false pretences or to find ways in which people can avoid immigration officials. Many are aware of the increased security in the United States post 9/11. Before these measures were introduced, the Irish found many ways to evade detection as they entered and left the United States while they were undocumented. This is becoming increasingly difficult now.

The second tool is shifting the responsibility onto airlines and shipping companies to ensure that people have the right visas. Large fines are placed on these carriers if they transport someone without a valid visa or entry permit. The recent Asylum and Immigration Act in Britain in 1999 extended the legislation to include drivers of trucks, whether they were aware of migrants in their vehicles or not.

The third tool is the detention of Asylum Seekers in prison-like conditions, to discourage people from making the journey in the first place. In recent years some countries set up off-shore detention centres to provide temporary accommodation to those seeking asylum. Australia is one country that pursued this option and it developed a policy whereby they paid poorer neighbouring countries to 'house' asylum seekers while they were being processed. Not setting foot in Australian territory, the Australian authorities deemed that they had no duty or obligation towards those seeking asylum. Many human rights groups have decried both the location and the philosophy behind these centres to no avail. One of the locations chosen by Australia was Manus Island in Papua New Guinea (PNG). However a recent decision of the Supreme Court in PNG ruled that the 'processing centre' was illegal, and in breach of the country's constitution.

A similar mind-set in Ireland created the direct provision centres that house those seeking asylum. It can be easy to point the finger at injustices committed in other countries and fail to see the shortcomings in one's own country. A recent report to the Minister for Justice entitled *Working Group to Report to Government Working Group on the Protection Process on Improvements to the Protection Process, including Direct Provision and Supports to Asylum Seekers*, was presented to the Minister in June 2015[15]. The report noted that many of the centres were run by private companies unlike other countries where such centres were run by not-for-profits who reinvested any surpluses into the accommodation. Twenty three percent of residents were detained in these sites for up to one year with 43.5% detained for five years or more. The recommendation of the report highlighted the shortcomings of these direct provision centres. Indeed the report notes that many of the rules and regulations of the centres are in fact just plain illegal[16]. Recommendations like the right to cooking facilities, the right to a private room (80% of people are in shared rooms, each room accommodating from two, up to eight, people)[17]. Children complained of hunger and often the kitchen opening hours meant that the children continuously ate reheated food when they returned from school[18]. The referral rates for child protection and child welfare issues was considerably higher for children in direct provision than the referral rate for the general child population[19]. On another important note, the mixed centres were deemed inappropriate for those who were victims of sex trafficking or sexual violence[20].

A country has the right to protect its borders and to offer security to its citizens, but what is happening in our country is in keeping with international trends. Horrific injustices happen on our doorsteps and in our name. As one person responded when asked what should be done: 'Damage has already been done – lives have been damaged – release people from direct provision – personalities have been damaged.' [21]

The subtle message of these centres is that we (Government) will make life worse for you than life in the place you have left, which is in keeping with the third tool to deter inward migration.

The overarching narrative then is one of deterrence. Granted, there has to be security to protect borders, but this right to security needs to also apply to displaced people; people whose reason for fleeing the place into which they are born is often due to unrest caused by the policies of countries external to their homeland, as recent history has shown us. Confusion on this issue abounds because of competing narratives with regard to migration and migrants. One could spend many pages highlighting some of the contradictions that abound in migration policy. In summary, it's not that countries want to stop migration; it is that they want to stop certain kinds of migrants. We are all aware that much of the wealth in western countries is brought about by the movement of capital and of certain categories of people. Within all the powerful narratives that dominate and describe the world of migration, one narrative that deserves to be heard is the one proclaimed by the Church. The rich tradition and teaching of the Church on this matter is seldom heard, even from the voices of our Church leaders who sometimes prefer the language of state and human rights, which undervalues the deeper unifying message of God's love for the stranger. One powerful voice is that of Pope Francis, who used the richness of the Church to speak on behalf of those who perished in the Mediterranean in April 2015:

> "A boat full of migrants capsized last night about 60 miles off the Libyan coast and hundreds are feared dead. I express my deepest sorrow in the face of this tragedy and I assure my thoughts and prayers to those still missing and to their families (…) These are men and women like us, our brothers and sisters seeking a better life, starving, persecuted, wounded, exploited, victims of war; they are seeking a better life. They were seeking happiness."[22]

If we are to fully understand our mission to migrants our mission has to reflect the tradition that influences Pope Francis in his powerful advocacy and actions on behalf of migrants.

MIGRATION AND CATHOLIC TEACHING TRADITION

For citizens of faith, such recognition is not an occasional glance but a habitual disposition or virtue, which the tradition names hospitality[23].

THE ROLE OF 'CHURCH' IN OUR PRESENT CRISIS

Migration today is a mirror to our Church, which exposes its flaws and highlights its strengths. The main flaw is the lack of leadership on this issue in the Irish Church. We have a number of statements but there is no coherent plan to effect change. There is no one who, like Pope Francis, has walked twelve people from a place of oppression and loss to a place of liberation and life. Despite a long tradition of action and service towards migrants and refugees in the Church, our voice today blends with those who seek to hold onto the status quo. There are strengths within the Church; a brief historical overview of the Irish Churches' response to Emigration shows vitality, expertise and commitment to the plight of those who have found themselves destitute abroad. People have opened their doors and await the arrival of someone to whom they can provide a home, yet no one arrives. Pastoral Councils in some parishes have identified spaces where people can live when they arrive, yet no one knocks.

There is a role for the Church in Ireland today to coordinate efforts on behalf of those whose lives are far from fulfilled and are placed in peril every day. There is a role to challenge the inaction of Government. There is a role to educate people as to the reasons why we must act. There is a role for the Church to close the gap that lies between the generosity of people who are willing to open their hearts and homes and those that are in such dire need. There is a role for the Church to be a Church and not another mediocre actor in civil society; in short the Church needs to rediscover itself in its mission to the stranger.

This message of Pope Francis is not one that is composed to engage with the present crisis; it is a message that lies at the heart of the Church's Social Teaching and is made explicit in a document published by EMCC in 2004, The Love of Christ for Migrants[1]. This document underlines the central mission of the Church in a world that is more diverse and pluralistic in its makeup.

For this reason the entire Church in the host country must feel concerned and engaged regarding immigrants. This means that local parishes must rethink pastoral care, programming it to help the faithful live their faith authentically in today's new multicultural and pluri-religious context.[24]

At the heart of the Church's teaching on migration is the supreme message that the task of assisting the migrant is not merely to serve social needs but that our service allows us to discover who we truly are as God's People. Deirdre Cornell was someone who set out to assist and give of herself and her bounty but her work led her on a different path.

She wrote of her experience working with migrants: 'I had unconsciously assumed that we were bringing the Church to migrants when it was *they* who also freely shared the Church with us'[25].

A brief overview of scripture will help us focus on this great truth.

THE OLD TESTAMENT

The Old Testament is full of stories. These stories are open to interpretation. In this section you are invited to take a brief overview of some of the characters of the Old Testament and their migratory status. However, you are also invited to look in more detail at the migratory status of one of the characters of the Old Testament. Many people today do not have the opportunity to explore scripture in detail. Hopefully this study will show you how our familiarity with stories from the Bible can discourage us from looking deeply into things and interpreting these stories in a manner that assists us in our various missions today. No Christian commentary on migration is complete without reference to the hand of God at work in people's lives.

When Moses was placed in a basket of rushes by his mother, it was a prophetic utterance. Centuries after this event we still see mothers placing their children on boats as they push their children towards spaces and places that cultivate hope and life. Moses was essentially the first refugee; a person without status fleeing for his life[26]. Too young to know, like many today, he found safety and he found life. However, we now know that his journey didn't end here. Leading the chosen people from Egypt he certainly freed them from slavery but as a result of this action they became strangers in new lands. They were strangers in Egypt and they were strangers as they sought out a land they could call home.

Before Moses comes to our attention in the Book of Exodus we find Abraham in the Book of Genesis. He was a man who set out on a journey not knowing his destination. A man who risked all in search of a new future believing that God would walk with him and guide him. He left the familiarity and stability of life in Ur travelling onto Haran and then onto Egypt. There were many epic events, but the one that speaks deepest to the spirituality and theology of migration is the one of the three visitors to the tent of Abraham and Sarah, his wife, in a place called Mamre. The welcome they provided is a paradigm for Christian welcome; from this moment of welcome they received great grace and blessings, which allowed Abraham become the father of a great nation. This nation has given birth to three great world faiths, Judaism, Islam and Christianity. The home, a simple tent, which was open to strangers represented a heart that was open to God's grace and God's mission for the world. 'Bowing down with his face touching the ground, he (Abraham) said, "Sirs, please do not pass by my home without stopping, I am here to serve you."(Gen 18:2) It was Clement of Rome in his Epistle to the Corinthians in 100 CE who noted that 'it is by faith and hospitality that Abraham became the son of the Covenant'[27].

Another great character of the Old Testament that we find in the Book of Genesis is Joseph, who was forced into slavery in Egypt by his jealous brothers. Joseph was the preferred son of his father, Jacob, something that is represented by his 'long coat of many colours'. At first, he suffered as a slave but eventually, and due to a series of events that revealed good luck and divine intervention, he became a trusted servant of the space called the Egyptian nation. When his brothers came to him many years later seeking his support due to their poverty stricken state, we are told that 'Joseph could no longer control his feelings. No one else was with him when he told his brothers who he was. He cried such loud sobs that the Egyptians heard it and the news was taken to the King's palace.' (Gen 45:1-2)

Joseph the migrant, despite all his worldly gains, acknowledged his human losses. Fortune smiled on him. From the status of a trafficked person, a slave, an indentured labourer he rose to a position of power and influence. Having undergone this trauma due to his siblings' jealousy, he was a refugee in Egypt and had to accept the limitations of his situation. Though he excelled, his Hebrew origins meant that he was never fully accepted into the life of the court; he reached what we now call 'a glass ceiling'[28]. It is often the case that migrants reach similar obstacles in their new countries. Joseph is an example of someone who was held back by the society that gave him a home. This is similar in many ways to today's world where people are inhibited from reaching their potential due to various classifications. There are many justifications for these policy tools but it is still hard on the one who, like Joseph, seeks only to excel. In Joseph's case this was due to his racial background; for others in the world today various classifications have been created to protect the interests of those who came first to various spaces and now occupy them. They put many obstacles in place to protect their status, which in turn act as glass ceilings for those who are newly arrived. Many Irish emigrants met such obstacles in the past. For instance, Irish emigrants were employed as indentured labourers to build the levies in New Orleans. The local landowners chose not to assign their slaves to this task as they were too valuable. If a slave died, the landowner lost someone who had many years left to give to his 'master'; if an Irish emigrant died in the levy, he could be replaced the next day without cost.

Elsewhere in the Old Testament, we find people who cross borders and enter new spaces, which on occasion brings new and exciting opportunities and on other occasions brings on a form of imprisonment. One complex example lies in the story of Ruth. Her story is most often associated with weddings as the reading 'Wherever you go, I shall go' is chosen by couples to depict loyalty and fidelity. The readings conceal a story ravaged by disloyalty and infidelity. Furthermore Ruth is always the outsider. As a Moabite, and not an Israelite, she faced estrangement in Israel and could not become a fully integrated member of the community in which she lived. Her mother-in law Naomi, along with her husband Elimelech, and their two sons were Israelites in exile in Ruth's hometown of Moab. Their exile was caused by a famine in Bethlehem. While the family were in Moab and during this exile, Ruth married their son Mahlon. Ruth's sister married Mahlon's brother Kilion. For Ruth, marrying a Hebrew migrant opened new opportunities and the hope of a better life. Tragically, all three women ended up as widows and Naomi was left with little option but to travel back to Bethlehem, her original home place. She encouraged Ruth and Orpah to remain in Moab, but only Orpah remained. Ruth travelled on to Bethlehem with her mother-in-law. This was the journey that inspired the words mentioned earlier, which are often used at weddings namely, 'wherever you go, I will go'.

These words were scribed not to underline the strength of a matrimonial relationship but to define a relationship of sorts between a widow and her mother-in-law, who was also a widow!

Much has been written about these verses. Some of these writings highlight the virtue of marriage but there are many scholars who may not subscribe to the overly romantic interpretation of this text. Scripture scholars believe that the relationship was less of love and more one of exploitation and necessity[29]. Naomi as an elderly widow had no one to look after her. At her age it was highly unlikely that she could get married, the objective was to arrange for Ruth to marry someone who would support them both. Ruth was a young attractive female without a protector and needed Naomi's status as an Israelite to gain a foothold in her new society. It was Naomi who suggested the romantic meeting between Ruth and Boaz and her plan worked. Whether she was closer to a match-maker or a sex trafficker is a topic for discussion, but whatever her role was it was not one of passivity as she was actively involved in the seduction of Boaz. Many depictions of sex traffickers today are depictions of criminals, the tough rugged type; this is not always the case. The story of Ruth and Naomi shows a form of trafficking that is supported by a family.

Furthermore, Ruth is no doubt an illegal alien in Israel and also a migrant worker exposed to menial labour, until her beauty is used by herself, but primarily by Naomi, to escape from this servitude. The story is not primarily one of undying love but one that tells of a series of exploitations of people who are displaced and without status. The efforts of both Naomi and Ruth echo the words of Pope

Francis when he spoke to the European Parliament in November 2014 when he said; 'The boats landing daily on the shores of Europe are filled with men and women who need acceptance and assistance'[30]. The Book of Ruth could be a story based in our world today as it relates a story of marginalised individuals who were made to realise that once they gained formal acceptance, assistance followed. Once Ruth was formally married her social acceptance allowed both herself and Naomi receive the assistance they required to live well.

This short overview of the Old Testament has highlighted that Moses, Abraham and Joseph, all leading figures in the history of salvation, were people who were migrants. It was while they were on their individual migratory journeys that God's plan was made known to them individually and also to the People of God. The overview also outlined the migratory nature of Ruth's story. Every one of these characters, in their own unique way, played their part in keeping the Davidic Line in place. The Davidic Line is the bloodline of Jesus, and is traced back to Abraham (Mt 1:2-17). The story of Ruth reveals that God's plan can be kept alive in the most marginalised of people and not in the vestibules of power. This may appear strange until we give consideration to the socio-economic status and culture of the family who brought the Child Jesus into the world.

THE NEW TESTAMENT

The document EMCC highlights four elements of the New Testament's relevance to migrants. Firstly, it tells us that Jesus was born into the world as a foreigner and, secondly, that he moved through the countryside of Judea venturing into towns and villages on his own. Thirdly, the document focuses on the person of Mary, who can be seen as the 'living symbol' of the migrant as she gave birth away from home and upon giving birth had to flee to Egypt. Fourthly, the document presents the Feast of Pentecost as a new dispensation when distinctions between peoples and races are dissolved. The vision of Pentecost holds before us that we are all migrants journeying to our heavenly home, which is our only true home. Furthermore, we are told that diversity is more the norm in life as it is a reminder to us of the universality of the Church and the universality of Her mission.

When the Word was made flesh that flesh was migrant flesh: the flesh of a refugee; the flesh of a displaced person and the flesh of an undocumented person. The Word took flesh in the dust and grime of life; far from the polished stone of the Jerusalem temple.

To fully appreciate the New Testament context for the migrant, one has to understand the cultural and social context of Jesus' life. Documents like EMCC look at how incidents mentioned in scripture relate to the migrant situation today, but there is a deeper resonance when one scratches beneath the surface. To fully understand the message of Jesus and how it applies to today's context, it is good to remind ourselves of one single and basic principle in theology and ecology, namely that that this earth is for everyone. The opening paragraph of Pope Francis' document commenting on the state of our world today, *Laudato Si*, tells us that 'Saint Francis of Assisi reminds us that our common home is like a sister with whom we share our life and a beautiful mother who opens her arms to embrace us'[31]. It is only a naïve person who would contemplate a world without borders and divides; however, they do not have to be as destructive, divisive and abusive as they often are. Neither should they be used to propose that one part of the globe is more entitled to the fruits of the earth than any other part.

A lot of the focus in the Gospels is on Jesus's journey to Jerusalem, the city which was the centre of power in Judea and where he was eventually arrested, tried, sentenced and crucified by the authorities of that city. Jerusalem, though it had a variety of peoples within its walls, was essentially a homogenous society where the religious and civil bodies worked together to maintain their positions of privilege and authority. The Jewish aristocratic elite worked hand in hand with the Roman authorities to exploit and dominate their own people. This was very different from the place that Jesus grew up in. Scriptural studies by Joseph Meier, Sean Freyne and Virgil Elizondo among others testify to the humble Galilean origins of Jesus as a key formative influence on his persona and thoroughly in keeping with the mission of the Kingdom of God[32].

The Gospels mention Galilee or the Galileans more than sixty times. Capernaum is one of those places in Galilee that gives valuable insight into the culture that surrounded Jesus until he made his way towards Jerusalem. Every one of us can identify with how the place we grew up in influenced the way we act in the world and how we think the world should be. Similarly with Jesus, Galilee influenced his thoughts and actions in the world. Capernaum was the total opposite to Jerusalem. The city of Jerusalem stood as a monolithic centre of power, Capernaum was a frontier where Jewish villagers met with diverse populations, some visiting, some trading and some plundering. Its location meant it had witnessed plundering warlords and the subsequent instability over the centuries resulting in a situation whereby:

"The inhabitants were mostly poor, rural peasants exploited by distant landowners, impure, rebellious, and ignorant. Many negative stereotypes about the Galilean Jews abounded, and despite their love and loyalty to Jerusalem and the Temple, they were despised among some elites who lived there."[33]

It would not have been unusual for the inhabitants of Galilee to travel for work, and at times they may even have been conscripted to work on projects by the foreign forces. Unlike Jerusalem, which was strong and defendable, Capernaum was porous and open to plunder. This was reflected in their world of ideas as well. Galileans had to absorb diverse peoples and ideas as it was a frontier region for Israel and had many borders. Diverse encounters were part of their everyday experience. Though they had seen many invasions, most of their encounters forged bonds of friendship and hospitality, which encouraged trade and commerce. However this history also brought with it a knowledge of the suffering that can be caused by unjust social and political structures.

It was because he was a Galilean that Jesus knew rejection, and why he found the Pharisees more difficult to deal with than the Samaritans. He instinctively knew that what was strange was not necessarily dangerous and that those who are excluded can often be the opportunity for new possibilities in a stale and sterile society. Even at a business level it was the energy, diversity and movement in Capernaum that gave it an ability to make money allowing its inhabitants to prosper. Furthermore, he knew that the God of people's hearts helped them to hold onto their identity when challenged by diverse surroundings. In the face of his upbringing in Galilee and despite its diversity, Jesus 'died a pious Jew reciting the evening prayer of his people, placing hope and confidence in the God who saves'[34].

Furthermore, in the Post-Resurrection narratives we hear that the disciples are sent from Galilee to the nations of the world; they are not sent as representatives of Jerusalem power brokers, but as servants of a new vision for the People of God. The rejected one starts His mission among the most rejected while proclaiming a universal message of welcome and peace. His clarion cry for a disordered world that denies equality to all is rejection. This vision is to be seen 'not as deficient but as pregnant with multiple possibilities for a broader, more generous future for all'[35].

The New Testament's instruction on migration cannot be limited merely to kindly deeds or just developing a sense of empathy with migrants. The New Testament asks us to start in a place of displacement and to see the world from Galilee rather than Jerusalem. It is such a place that inspires Pope Francis to write words such as these for the World Day for Migrants and Refugee, 2014:

"A change of attitude towards migrants and refugees is needed on the part of everyone, moving away from attitudes of defensiveness and fear, indifference and marginalisation – all typical of a 'throwaway culture' – towards attitudes based on a culture of encounter, the only culture capable of building a better, more just and fraternal world."[36]

It is words like this that bring the wisdom of the past into the present to help us face the challenge of today's migrations.

HOSPITALITY

Over the last number of years, the Church has given priority to migration and migrants. Largely this is due to the voice of Pope Francis, who sees in the eyes of the migrant all that is wrong with our world today. The Pope has the assistance of The *Pontifical Council for Migrants and Itinerant People*, which was set up in 1988 and which was subsequently absorbed into the *Pontifical Council for Justice and Peace* at a later date[37]. Every year there is a *World Day for Migrants and Refugees* for which the Pope prepares a document, usually in the previous September, which is circulated widely in advance so local Churches can absorb and act on the sentiments of the message. In Ireland the *World Day for Migrants and Refugees* often overlaps with *Church Unity Octave Week* and so gets little, if any, attention. To help to understand the richness of the Church's message on migration and its relevance to today's challenges, a consideration of the Church's teaching will be viewed through the lens of the United States Conference of Catholic Bishops (USCCB) and the Mexican Catholic Bishops Conference (CEM). Finally, a tradition that has been in existence for over 1,500 years in Europe will assist in our understanding of the Church's understanding of hospitality.

In ecclesial jurisdictions outside of Ireland, many Churches are leaders in the work of advocating for migrants and refugees and in supporting projects for integration. An example of this is a living reality in the United States where the Bishops Conference in the United States and Mexico issued a joint pastoral entitled *Strangers No Longer; Together on a Journey of Hope*[38]. Using the tradition of the Church, this document presents five principles, which are seen as emerging from the Church's Social Teaching. The first principle is: *Persons have a right to find opportunities in their own land.* In summary this means that people first and foremost have a right not to migrate; they have a right to stay in the place where they were born and there cultivate a life in a familiar environment with family and friends by their side. This basic right is stolen because of poverty, violence, war, environmental change, natural disasters and a basic lack of opportunity.

Secondly *people have a right to migrate to support themselves and their families.* Migration was in the blood of the earliest civilisations. They migrated to fertile places avoiding the impact of changing seasons and always in the name of survival. Many indigenous peoples continue this practise today. Poverty may be defined as the lack of choice; on many occasions people are forced to migrate because they have no choice; this is different to people who choose to migrate because they are making a life-style decision. At the heart of migration policy is the challenge to distinguish between those who are forced to leave their home because they have no choice and those who choose to leave something behind because they perceive there is something better elsewhere.

The third principle is that *sovereign nations have a right to control their borders.* There are many who advocate for open borders, indeed as we discussed earlier the border between the UK and Ireland was an open border over the centuries. The introduction of visa-based travel is in effect a border enforcement strategy that puts a barrier between those who enter a country and those who decide who should enter a country. The objective of these measures is to protect the fabric and cohesion of that nation. A society is not something that is constructed overnight; it is something that evolves and has to be nurtured. One definition of social cohesion is 'the ability of a society to so coordinate its resources as to produce what it needs to sustain and reproduce itself'[39]. The challenge of migration and latterly integration is to bring about a climate where diversity does not mean divisiveness but encourages human and societal flourishing.

Fourthly, their publication states that *refugees and asylum seekers should be afforded protection.* This was dealt with in an earlier section but it does underline the important role of the global community when other communities experience traumatic conditions that render them homeless and stateless. The document underlines that they should be able to claim refugee status 'without incarceration'.

The fifth and final principle refers to undocumented migrants. It states that *the human dignity and the human rights of undocumented migrants should be respected.* This is a particular point of concern for the American and Mexican Churches, however it is a matter of growing concern for many nations throughout the world including Ireland. As was stated earlier, the need for a visa has created a potential for illegal or undocumented migrants in many jurisdictions. In summary, regardless of a person's status, that person still possesses a human dignity and a Christian dignity that overrides their legal status and out of which basic human rights flow.

These five principles highlight that the document is written in an aspirational way but is heavily underlined with a note of realism. The reason there is such a strong commitment to migration is that both the United States and the Mexican Bishop's Conferences view migration as an undeniable sign and characteristic of the times we live in and this is strongly encouraged by our policies of globalisation. They also show us how the Church's social teaching provides a valid framework for policy that is in keeping with the overarching demands of a cohesive society. Hospitality is an essential part of cohesion and if there is no dialogue with new things and new people, communities will diminish and eventually die.

Speaking of the challenges facing the modern world, the sociologist Zygmunt Bauman says that: 'It is a neighbourhood of meandering, spongy and porous boundaries in which it is difficult to ascertain who legally belongs and who is a stranger, who is at home and who is an intruder'[40].

This is an issue today but it is also an issue throughout the history of civilisation and has been an issue for communities since the earliest times. Indeed, much of what we mentioned in our sections on the Old and New Testaments revealed these tensions. We would love to lock ourselves away at times and feel secluded and protected from the ever-increasing madness of the world, but that is not an option. Change, and the challenge of change, always faces us as individuals, communities and as societies. The question that arises is: has anyone dealt with diversity in a positive way in our history; has any group managed to survive while holding its doors and hearts open to the stranger?

There is one such example in answer to the last question, namely, the Benedictine Order, which has existed in Europe for over 1500 years. Hospitality is one of their vows and it is seen as a sacred duty. In a world presently dominated by words, hospitality within Benedictine Communities is a communication by gesture. However hospitality is full of ambivalence; full of mixed feelings and even anxiety. The origins and use of the word *hospitality* alert us to this. The word *host* is at the root of the words hospitality, hostility and hostages; these three words are certainly ambivalent when placed alongside one another[41]. Even the Latin roots of the words reveal the challenge involved in receiving the guest. The *hospes* and *hostes* are similar sounding but the former means guest and the latter, enemy.

The whole process of welcoming and hospitality is a process of discerning whether the people or persons being welcomed add to the quality of the home or society into which they are welcomed, or whether they will disrupt the positive atmosphere that has been nurtured over the years. In societal terms, this management of hospitality is called integration. The French philosopher Jacques Derrida points out that the host is always in a position of power over the guest. What is crucial is how the welcoming community uses its position of power to create a welcome that leads to cohesive integration. This is particularly true for the Christian who is asked to see this process as having a divine impetus, namely that God is at the heart of the mission and is to be found in the process. In summary then, for a person of faith, hospitality is not just a series of kind deeds, but a habitual disposition within our tradition that nurtures and creates a space for encounter and discernment. Hospitality is:

"...primarily the creation of free space where the stranger can enter and become a friend instead of an enemy. Hospitality is not to change people but to offer them space where change can take place. It is not to bring men and women over to outside, but to offer freedom not disturbed by dividing lines. It is not to lead our neighbour into a corner where there are no alternatives left, but to open a wide spectrum of options for choice and commitment (…) To convert hostility into hospitality requires the creation of the friendly empty space where we can reach out to our fellow human beings and invite them to a new relationship."[42]

This is indeed a mighty challenge that involves a degree of discomfort for everyone, especially the host who is asked to go beyond oneself in love and acceptance of the other. However, it was never meant to be easy. The way that the world has been constructed by the neo-liberals, who favour economic outcomes over social or communitarian outcomes, sees a trend towards reaping the benefits of the unequal worlds that we have come to know as the First and Third Worlds. People who see the world in this way may find the Christian challenge unsettling to say the least. This is not to undervalue the creation of wealth; it just raises questions as to how it is raised and how it is distributed. Fr Jim Keenan puts it well when he says that true Christian hospitality involves entering into the chaos of another's life[43] – and chaos is never comfortable. What Abraham, Moses, Joseph, Ruth, Naomi, and indeed Jesus were asked to do was not comfortable by any means. In a particular way Jesus was asked to step into the chaos of our lives and indeed he still does to this day. It is in him that we find our inspiration and strength as we look at how our communities can aid welcome and integration.

MIGRATION AND THE LOCAL
FAITH COMMUNITY

*It was the economist Amartya Sen who first recognised
that poverty is, fundamentally; not the debt of money or
a lack of possessions or a shortage of talent or ambition,
but the lack of capacities – the lack of opportunities
needed to function as a full citizen.*[44]

*And what arrival cities need most – and what the market
will almost never provide – are the tools to become
normal urban communities.*[45]

On a recent visit to Lampedusa, an island off the coast
of Libya, I met people who give support to migrants res-
cued from the Mediterranean and brought to the shore. A
portion of the pier is set aside as a refugee centre and lo-
cals have no automatic right to access the area when the
refugees arrive. On occasion, however, the military or the
coast guard permitted access. The heart-breaking stories
that I heard from people who walked among the refugees,
mostly women and children, were humbling to say the
least. One sister told of a time when she went among the
migrants with bottles of water, pouring it into their hands
so they could refresh themselves. Remember, having been
at sea for a few days, the people were starved of food and
water supplies. On one occasion a mother reached for-

ward, the sister thinking that the mother was looking for water drew the bottle back slightly but the mother only wanted to touch the cross that was around her neck. She held the cross even though she had a great thirst as she thanked God for the safe arrival of her family to the shore.

The most stunning memories of the visit, were the times when those who provided assistance talked about looking in the eyes of migrants. As we listened to these stories, one realised that these were moments of deep encounter when those providing assistance saw fear in the eyes, hearts and souls of the migrants. What is noticeable about current polices in the EU and especially among those responsible for taking refugees into Ireland is the obvious way they are putting everything in place to ensure that people cannot look into the eyes of those who arrive. In many ways the policy and the language is that of dehumanisation. The segregation of people into camps in isolated areas, the silence surrounding numbers and placements, the discouragement of involvement by local communities, the gap between the goodness of people in terms of offerings of housing and hospitality, tells of policy decisions that aim to build walls between people and migrants. For any community who wishes to step forward and offer assistance, be aware that the institutions responsible for settling people will not want to engage.

Though there are many who want to offer assistance, many things will be made difficult for them. This policy comes from the top down and the evidence of this lies in the recent general election in Ireland. Though we claim to be European, little was spoken about in regard to the crisis that presently haunts the borders of Southern Europe. To be fair though, politics is tuned into the minds of people and follows what the populace want: there may be a large cohort of people who may not want migrants and refugees in their area, so the political volume was toned down on this issue. I put this view out there just to highlight that any groups who wish to offer support may find it difficult to get information and advice as to how one might go about offering this support. From a faith based perspective there is no national plan in place. The institutional Catholic Church has not made a stance on the matter and by its silence is supporting the building of walls which distance good people from the eyes of those in need. There are some countries in the world that run refugee programmes that involve settling people in parishes with the support of the local faith community, but this is not the case in Ireland. Therefore, anyone who wants to offer assistance at this level may need to liaise with one of Ireland's recognised agencies in order to offer and provide help. This should not be a source of discouragement but a source of resolve, as it is with many communities across Europe.

PRINCIPLES BEHIND THE LOCAL CHURCHES' MINISTRY TO MIGRANTS
PREPARING IN ADVANCE

There has been a lot of talk in Ireland about the numbers of refugees that Ireland will eventually take. The debate has, sadly, mostly been about numbers and there is a vast difference between what has been promised and what has been realised. In September 2015, the Minister for Justice promised to take 4,000 refuges into Ireland. However, as of Saint Patrick's Day 2016, only 261 refugees had arrived into Ireland[46]. Nevertheless, it is important for faith communities to prepare for the arrival of people who seek a new home. No time is wasted in this preparation. I remember when Ireland hosted the Special Olympics in 2003, a lot of preparation was undertaken by the Host Towns before people arrived into homes and communities. This preparation meant that the engagements were more uplifting and enriching. As stated earlier, the aim of this booklet is to provide some background information and reflections to assist communities and their leaders as they prepare to receive migrants and refugees. The information provided thus far will help a community locate their mission of care and support within the broader mission of the Church. This work is not just a work that occurs on the margins of the Churches' mission but one that is intrinsically a part of her mission.

PROVIDING INFORMATION

Advance work could be done preparing booklets with basic information in the various languages that someone might need when they arrive. I notice in my work that even though people may have a good grasp of English, there are often technical terms that they may not understand. There are things like cuts of meat, local landmarks, bus routes and other forms of public transport that may need to be translated into English. Photographs to accompany these would prove very helpful indeed. As one is aware from travelling abroad, the best guidebooks are full of local information. During the first week of college, students do not think about graduation in four years' time; they just want to find the classroom for the next class!

UNDERSTANDING

Any knowledge that can be collated about the country where people have travelled from is to be welcomed. This can be done well in advance and could even be part of a local school project. Despite all the preparations for the arrival of groups for the Special Olympics, there were always those awkward moments when people arrived in your home. Irish people know what it is like for people to work from caricatures of the quintessential Irish person. A friend of mine who does not drink alcohol was welcomed in an Arab country as 'the first Irish Muslim' that had visited the person's home. No matter how many briefings the communities had, one question was vital when meeting visitors from other cultures and, indeed, it is a question I use to this day, simply put it starts with 'Help me to understand … ' This could refer to eating habits, washing habits, prayers habits, family customs, national celebrations etc. This simple question is an open one that translates into engagement and trust if the answer is heard and understood.

BOUNDARIES

It is essential to provide guidelines for boundaries and to ensure that child protection guidelines are in place for everyone involved in this work. Anyone who has spent time in refugee camps or has made hazardous journeys may have encountered traumatic events, which may only come to light when they begin to settle down. It would be a good idea to canvass the services of local counsellors, nurses, child psychologists and doctors who will be able to work together to help a person overcome the various difficulties that may come to light. It is often a medical visit that brings attention to other traumas, indicating that further interventions are required. I have dealt with a person who arrived in Ireland as a refugee. He cannot be near water as it brings to mind all his friends who drowned crossing the Mediterranean; despite the beautiful summers he cannot bring his family to the beach. His children do not understand his trauma but it is affecting them all, as they cannot enjoy this simple family pleasure. If these professionals are part of the process of induction then they will be tuned into the services that the refugees can avail of. As a chaplain in a third level institution I find that, working hand in hand with other professional services, it is often a simple gestures of inclusion that can help a person journey towards recovery alongside the other professional interventions.

Any initiative by a local community should involve familiarisation with organisations that have a proven track record in refugee and migrant care. Many of these organisations have developed good programmes of resettlement and have a great store of wisdom that should not be wasted or ignored. A great debt of gratitude is owed to many religious orders and communities who inspired, and at often times funded, the setting up of these groups when refugees and migrants started arriving into Ireland many years ago. These groups can be helpful but they are still limited in what they can do. The strongest agent of integration is the local community and especially kindly neighbours. The organisations that offer support depend on funding for their programmes so oftentimes they are not as responsive as they would like to be or ought to be due to a lack of funding and resources.

FAMILIARISATION

Any initiative by a local community should involve familiarisation with organisations that have a proven track record in refugee and migrant care. Many of these organisations have developed good programmes of resettlement and have a great store of wisdom that should not be wasted or ignored. A great debt of gratitude is owned to the religious orders and communities who inspired, and often times funded, the setting up of these groups when refugees and migrants started arriving into Ireland many years ago. While these groups can be helpful, they are still limited in what they can do. The strongest agent of integration is the local community and especially kindly neighbours. The organisations that offer support depend on funding for their programmes so if they are not as responsive as they'd like to be, or ought to be, it is often due to a lack of funding and resources.

LOCAL PROGRAMME OPTIONS

Regardless of the effort put into migration by national policy and programmes, people settle in local communities. A lot has been written about the best starting point for newly arrived people. Some research outlines the advantages and disadvantages of populating areas with people from the same sending country, who preserve their culture by cultivating a feeling of home-away-from-home. Others refer to this as 'ghettoisation'. Some policies suggest that people from the same sending country should not be settled in one location, instead placed in various locations in the host country. There are advantages and disadvantages to both and research bears this out. One disadvantage for people placed in the one location is that they may be slower to develop the language of their new home. On the other hand, one advantage of people living in the one area is that they set up small businesses thus creating a future for themselves and their families. There is no doubt that people from overseas, especially those who have left a conflict zone, like to meet to share updates and news from their homeland. One can conclude that no matter where people are given accommodation they will always connect with people with whom they share a common home.

One only has to look at city centre parishes in Dublin that provide culturally sensitive liturgies to observe the manner in which people gather to share stories and customs; not unlike the way Irish people gathered at the Oblate Father's in Kilburn where they found support for their Irish traditions. It was there that many gathered to attend Mass on Sundays and to buy Irish Sunday newspapers, hear how the local GAA team were doing and to catch up on news from home. These tendencies show that people have a natural desire to connect that overrides the intention of policies. Any local community that offers to support and engage with newly arrived people should not only be aware of this fact, but they should actively support it. The desire to be with others is in no way a denigration of the new community and its people. It is just what we do; in the midst of all that is new we crave the familiar. Regardless of category, newly arrived people live in a dislocated space; the balance between familiarity with their own culture and the kindness of a new community heals any sense of dislocation over time. The aim of welcome is not to force a person to forget their past but to live securely in the present. The question is how can we assist in this task?

One need not be frightened by the challenges associated with this task. Think of all the welcomes we have extended in our lives. New children may have come into our homes as babies. We nurtured them and gave them life. We have moved into neighbourhoods and opened our doors and hearts to neighbours who have become friends. Many of you reading this have in the past set up organisations, committees and clubs that have welcomed people who are now part of the fabric of our lives. One of the most natural instincts in the human being is to welcome others; we've just got to trust it and work with our instincts. The things that inhibit this natural instinct are fear, a lack of understanding and the opinion of others who may not share your value system. All these things can be overcome with a little knowledge, a modicum of belief and a lot of what we call 'community', i.e. people with whom we share common values and beliefs.

The first task that any community has is to identify new arrivals to the community. Sadly those administering the settlement of refugees are not always working with local communities to the degree that facilitates positive local integration. In an ideal world government agencies and non-governmental agencies would connect with local faith communities to link with new families. Meeting people before they arrive and creating a humanitarian corridor of welcome and settlement would reduce the feelings of strangeness, discomfort and alienation for everyone. Ideally, an advanced sponsoring programme, where communities get an opportunity to meet people before they arrive, would be helpful all round. Sadly this will not happen without the proper advocacy.

Once a family has arrived and been identified by a local support group, the tasks are very straightforward and obvious. In keeping with the thinking of *Erga Migrantes*, there is always a 'First Welcome', which is different in nature and substance to the ongoing welcome that leads towards integration. The initial welcome may include things like warm, waterproof clothing, an introduction to shopping facilities, doctor's surgeries, identification of faith communities in keeping with the background of the families, information on public transport and generally how to access services. Charts outlining rates of exchange with currencies that people previously used are very important. These can be accompanied with a list of prices of an average shopping basket of items, with photographs of the items, including utilities. As time evolves, people can be introduced to sports clubs and social facilities but one must keep in mind that customs surrounding changing and washing facilities may need particular sensitivity. If the local parish centre has a coffee shop or, failing this, the local coffee shop where people socialise, the management can be advised to stock items that are in keeping with the eating habits of the newly arrived family, especially the children. Basic research will reveal particular ingredients for dishes from their country of origin. If the local shop is unable to stock these supplies, then one could identify where the items could be bought in the many ethnic stores that are emerging in some Irish cities. Another important element of integration that a community group can help with is to organise a social gathering with the local Community Garda. We often forget that the sight of a uniform can instil terror into people especially if they have come from areas of conflict. Our society generally teaches us to trust a person in a uniform, but in some countries this is not the case. As already alluded to previously, the reason why many people leave their homeland is not necessarily poverty, but more likely a lack of justice and security, and an unlikelihood of any improvement in these conditions in the future.

Familiarisation with the country of origin of the new arrivals should include identifying feast days and national celebrations of the sending and receiving countries. While people can be introduced to the way we celebrate birthdays and anniversaries in Ireland, account should be taken of the manner and understanding of these celebrations in the family's own culture and traditions. The internet and the world of television and cinema have shown many people how feasts such as Christmas, Easter and New Year are celebrated in the western world. Even Christians from other parts of the world, however, may celebrate these events differently. We only have to think about how Saint Patrick's Day is marked abroad and how this celebration allows many Irish people to feel recognised and respected, even proud of their heritage.

Research shows us that immigrant groups place a great value on education. A welcoming group in the local faith community should provide an overview of the education system and how it can be accessed and what is expected in terms of behaviour and how parents and students interact with teachers and those in authority. The progression pathway through the education system ought to be outlined with particular attention paid to hidden costs in the system. As we know only too well, describing the Irish education system as 'free' may not be an accurate portrayal of the reality as many items and extra-curricular activities have to be paid for.

A key element in education is language skills. Some may have good English but this may only be spoken English. When immigration into Australia was at its height, people could avail of unlimited English language support in local libraries. A parish group should pay particular attention to women's English language ability. Many immigrant women choose to become homemakers, or their culture insists that they take on this role, and thus they may have less opportunity for language development as the default positon in their home is to speak in the language of their home country. Anyone who has worked in schools over the last few decades in Ireland is all too aware of situations whereby children have to interpret conversations between parents and teachers.

In summary, the welcome provided is based on our instinct with a little bit of sensitivity and understanding. We receive many visitors in our lives and we strive to make things easy for them; the same general rules apply to those who come to Ireland as refugees or forced migrants. The best source of information on the culture of those coming to our shores is the people themselves; assumptions that we make can add to the difficulty that a person experiences as they try to settle into their new home. When Jesus crossed borders and engaged with people he never made assumptions; he stepped outside cultural blind spots and looked into the eyes of those he met and liberated them through his belief in the love that his Father has for the entire human family.

CONCLUSION

But we need only take a frank look at the
facts to see that our common home
is falling into serious disrepair.
Hope would have us recognise that
there is always a way out, that we
can always redirect our steps,
that we can always do something
to solve our problems[47].

When Pope Francis addressed the bishops of Italy in Florence on 10 November 2015, he said, 'we are not living in the era of change but in the change of an era'. Nowhere is this to be seen more clearly than in what is happening on the doorstep of Europe. Migrants arriving in their thousands tell us that everything is changing. Old certainties that kept us in our safe structures are collapsing and we have to find a way to respond. The inequality in the world is causing our common home to burst at its seams. No longer will people dwell in the shadow of death but they will endeavour to seek out pastures new. Generations of Irish have done this and now other nations have no choice but to try to do the same.

The first section of this booklet helped us see beyond the

terms and labels placed on people. As the world managed the movement of people from various places, it has tried to protect spaces that have more wealth and security than those places that people were travelling from. The world shapes the way we think and sometimes it draws us away from the goodness that beats deep within us. Studying the Old and New Testaments and a meagre amount of Church teaching on this reveals that there is another way of understanding our world. The Christian message is more than just giving a person charity from our abundance; the Christian message demands, now more than ever, that we see our world differently before it falls apart. One way to begin this journey is to look deep into the eyes of those who have lost everything to see what they have found to be important.

There is an underlying principle in scripture and tradition that is often ignored because we view these things from our place of stability and security. This principle is that most of the characters we have come to know and understand in scripture were migrants; people who were on journeys of hope. For some their hopes were realised beyond all expectations, for others their hopes were dashed. Much of this depended on the response of those who welcomed them.

The last section of this book focused on the strength and power of the community that can, if it so wishes, provide a welcome. A few ideas were shared but in essence what this booklet hopes to achieve is to evoke in each one a more open and hospitable disposition towards all that is different in the world. When our hearts are opened then it is easier to open our arms to others. Hopefully this will help us live more comfortably and at peace with one another.

NOTES

1   Umberto Eco, *Five Moral Pieces* (London: Secker and Warburg, 2001) p.95

2   http://www.vatican.va/roman_curia/pontifical_councils/migrants/documents/rc_pc_migrants_doc_20040514_erga-migrantes-caritas-christi_en.html =accessed July 13th 2016].

3   Pope Francis @Pontifex 6 June, 2016, 4am.

4   Zygmunt Bauman, *Culture in a Liquid Modern World* (Cambridge: Polity Press, 2011) p.44.

5   Michael Pye, *The Edge of the World; How the North Sea Made Us Who We Are* (London: Penguin-Random House, 2014) pp.77-78.

6   Irish Times, Generation Emigration, Life and Style, http://www.irishtimes.com/life-and-style/generation-emigration/life-abroad-emigrating-to-australia-was-the-best-decision-i-have-ever-made-1.2620813 =accessed 01/05/2016]

7   International Organisation for Migrants (IOM) April 2014 http://www.un.org/en/development/desa/population/pdf/commission/2014/system/Agenda%20item%204/IOM_Item4.pdf =accessed 12/06/2016]

8   Warsan Shire, 'Home', 2009 http://seekershub.org/blog/2015/09/home-warsan-shire/ =accessed 03/05/2016]

9   Patrcia Kennedy, *Welcoming the Stranger; Irish Migrant Welfare in Britain Since 1957*, (Dublin: Irish Academic Press, 2015) p.28.

10 Michael Dummett (2001) *On Immigration and Refugees*, (Oxford: Routledge, 2001) p.90

11 Ibid p.101

12 'The Day Britain took in 27,000 Refugees', Channel 4, http://blogs.channel4.com/snowblog/day-britain-27000-refugees/25733 =accessed 14/05/2016]

13 Quoted in Robert Kanigel, *On an Irish Island,* (New York: Random House, 2012) p.221

14 Michael Dummett, pp.125-26.

15 Department of Justice. Working Group to Report to Government Working Group on the Protection Process on Improvements to the Protection Process, including Direct Provision and Supports to Asylum Seekers. (2015) http://www.justice.ie/en/JELR/Report%20to%20Government%20on%20Improvements%20to%20the%20Protection%20Process,%20including%20Direct%20Provision%20and%20Supports%20to%20Asylum%20Seekers.pdf/Files/Report%20to%20Government%20on%20Improvements%20to%20the%20Protection%20Process,%20including%20Direct%20Provision%20and%20Supports%20to%20Asylum%20Seekers.pdf =accessed 18/05/2016]

16 Ibid e.g. 4.162

17 Ibid 4.80

18 Ibid 4.93

19 Ibid

20 Ibid 4.206

21 Ibid, Appendices p.311

22 Angelus Message 19 May 2015, Vatican City http://w2.vatican.va/content/francesco/en/angelus/2015/documents/papa-francesco_regina-coeli_20150419.html =accessed 23/05/2016]

23 William O'Neill, 'Christian Hospitality and Solidarity with the Stranger, in Kerwin and Jill Marie Gerschutz,(Ed) *And You Welcomed Me; Migration and Catholic Social Teaching*, (ML: Lexington Books, 2009) p.150

24 EMCC para 41

25 Deirdre Cornell, *Jesus Was a Migrant*, (New York: Orbis Books, 2014) p.61

26 This insight was shared with me by Rev. Professor Daniel Groody, CSC PhD, when I visited the campus a number of years ago. He is Associate Professor of Theology and the Director of Immigration Initiatives at the Institute for Latino Studies at the University of Notre Dame.

27 Pierre-François De Béthune, *By Faith and Hospitality; The Monastic Tradition as a Model for Interreligious Encounter* (Herefordshire: Gracewing, 2002) vii

28 A glass ceiling refers to an inherent prejudice that subtly puts barriers in the way of people who move upwards in an organisation due to colour, creed, gender etc.

29 I would like to acknowledge the Work of Fulata Moyo: 'Traffic Violations': Hospitality, Foreignness and Exploitation – a Contextual Biblical Study of Ruth' in *The Feminist Journal of Studies in Religion*, (2016)

30 The Visit of Pope Francis to the European Parliament in Strasbourg, 25 November 2014, https://w2.vatican.va/content/francesco/en/speeches/2014/november/documents/papa-francesco_20141125_strasburgo-parlamento-europeo.html

31 Pope Francis, Laudato Si, Vatican City, (2015) http://w2.vatican.va/content/francesco/en/encyclicals/documents/papa-francesco_20150524_enciclica-laudato-si.html =accessed 29/05/2016]

32 John P Meier *Rethinking the Historical Jesus*, (New York: Doubleday, 1991); Sean Freyne, *Jesus, a Jewish Galilean: A New Reading of the Jesus Story*, (New York: T and T Clark, 2004); Virgil Elizondo, *Galilean Journey: The Mexican Promise*, (New York: Maryknoll, 2002)

33 Virgil Elizondo, 'Jesus the Galilean Jew in Mestizo Theology', *Theological Studies,* 70 (2009) pp.271-72

34 Ibid p.273

35 Ibid p.278

36 World Day for Migrants and Refugees, 2014. http://w2.vatican.va/content/francesco/en/messages/migration/documents/papa-francesco_20130805_world-migrants-day.html =accessed 29/05/2016].

37 For a more comprehensive overview of the Churches' role in migration read Patricia Kennedy, *Welcoming the Stranger; Irish Migrants Welfare in Britain Since 1957* (Dublin: Irish Academic Press, 2015) pp.42-59.

38 USCCB (2002) Strangers No Longer; Together on a Journey of Hope, http://www.usccb.org/issues-and-action/human-life-and-dignity/immigration/strangers-no-longer-together-on-the-journey-of-hope.cfm =accessed 1/06/2016]

39 Bouma, Gary and Rod Ling, 'Religious Resurgence and Diversity and Social Cohesion in Australia' in J Nieuwenhuysen (Ed), *Social Cohesion in Australia,* (Melbourne: Cambridge University Press, 2007) p.80

40 Zygmunt Bauman p.36.

41 For further information on the origins of the word and a discussion on interfaith hospitality see, Pierre-Francios OSB De Béthune, *By Faith and Hospitality; The Monastic Tradition as a Model for Interreligious Encounter*, (Herefordshire: Gracewing, 2002)

42 Quoted in Jill Marie Gerschutz and Lois Ann Lorentzen, Integration Yesterday and Today: New Challenges for the United States and the Church IN Kerwin and Jill Marie Gerschutz (Ed) *And You Welcomed Me; Migration and Catholic Social Teaching*, (ML: Lexington Books, 2009) pp.127-128.

43 Paul Farmer 'Chaos in a Time of Cholera' in Michael Griffin and Jennie Weiss Block, (Ed*) In the Company of the Poor,* (NY: Orbis Books, 2013) p.129

44 Doug Saunders, *Arrival City*, (London: Windmill Books, 2010) p.280

45 Ibid p.310

46 Marie O'Hallaran, 'Ten Refugees out of Promised 2620 have arrived in Ireland' The Irish Times, 17 March 2016, available http://www.irish-times.com/news/politics/ten-refugees-out-of-promised-2-620-have-arrived-in-ireland-1.2576107 =accessed 06/06/2016]

47 Pope Francis, *Laudato Si*, (Vatican City, 2015) para 61

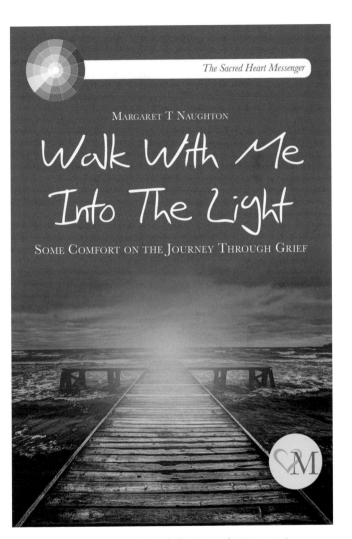

The Sacred Heart Messenger

Margaret T Naughton

Walk With Me Into The Light

Some Comfort on the Journey Through Grief

WWW.MESSENGER.IE
TEL: 01 7758522
€3.99

BEING THERE

A COMPANION ON THE PATHWAY OF ILLNESS

MARGARET T NAUGHTON

Author of *Walk With Me Into The Light: Some Comfort on the Journey Through Grief*

WWW.MESSENGER.IE
TEL: 01 7758522
€3.99

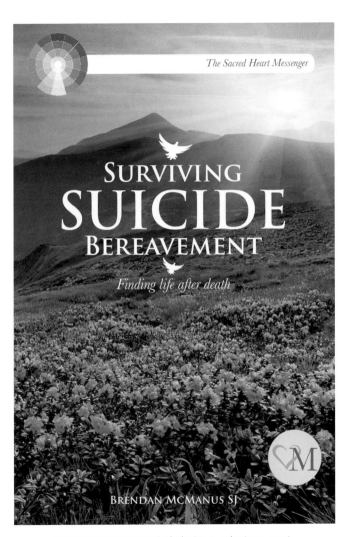

SURVIVING
SUICIDE
BEREAVEMENT

Finding life after death

BRENDAN MCMANUS SJ

WWW.MESSENGER.IE
TEL: 01 7758522
€3.99

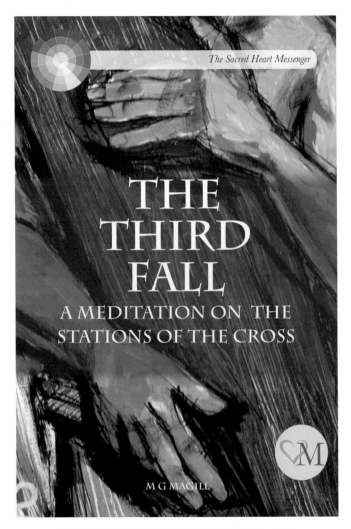

THE THIRD FALL

A MEDITATION ON THE STATIONS OF THE CROSS

M G MAGILL

WWW.MESSENGER.IE
TEL: 01 7758522
€3.99